D1527630

the last mile on the tanka road

the last mile on the tanka road

Sanford Goldstein

A Stark Mountain Press Book

the last mile on the tanka road

Starkmtpress@gmail.com

Acknowledgments are made to the editors of Tanka Society of America and Atlas Poetica where some of these poems have been published.

Cover photo – Sanford Goldstein on the road to Shibata-shi – by Kazuaki Wakui
© 2023

Cover design by Larry Kimmel

ISBN: 979-8-3936885-9-2
Imprint: Independently published

Rest in peace Sanford
and thank you for all you have done
for this tanka world

Larry

Foreword

I met Sanford Goldstein in person just once, in the 1970s at an Alan Watts lecture in Ottawa, when I lived in Toronto and he lived on the other side of Lake Ontario, in Ohio. Then our paths diverged and he moved to Japan to teach and I moved back to England and worked as a nurse.

I still followed his tanka road and gathered his books. More than three decades passed with struggles on both sides, and he retired to Shibata-shi and I became paraplegic after the crash and we connected again in the online tanka world and it was he who told me to submit my tanka(I had written them since the age of nine) to the journals. We became fast friends and wrote a lot of tanka together over the years which were published in various journals. We shared in daily emails, a lot of the sorrows and losses of both of our lives and often they crept into the tanka too.

Now at 97 he is too old to write anymore. But a couple of years ago, I promised him I would submit the later tanka he had sent me, and our unpublished strings, if he was not able. Then I got stopped by the loss of my daughter and now I need to honour his wish.

There are not many tanka, as he had slowed down as he grew old, and many of them are sad and dark as he looked back on his own losses. I hesitate, but Sandy("Joy, call me Sandy") always said that above all else tanka should tell the truth, and these last ones do.

You can find his life in tanka in many books, all of them amazing. We in the tanka world owe him a great debt.To me he is the most honest voice in tanka since the old Japanese poets.

I give thanks to Sandy's family for letting us share these last tanka, and also I give thanks to Sandy for being one of the best poets and best friends I have ever known. And gratitude to Kazuaki for his constant care of my old friend.

In these poems
there is the darkness
of age and loss
and yet ... still the shining
of the light of his courage

Joy McCall Norwich, 2023

tanka at the café

no place
to go for relief,
for sanity
I face my tanka notebook,
speak what I cannot say

my epiphany,
did it last even a night?
it is not clear –
what was it I felt then?
who were the main actors?

my English friend
knows the bitterness
of loss
how she has borne the pain
and mine has just started

a passerby
speaks to me
I am silent –
am I a cloistered monk?
do I have to eat food dished out?

all warm
in this winter coat
this winter hat
inwardly I am ablaze
with trapped thoughts

why must I stumble
carrying my old long-used cane
to the garbage site,
why must I sit in silence
over food I do not want?

how fierce
my looks these days
sculpted with anger
I want to erase these feelings
want to, even though I can't

too embittered
even for silent tears
to flow
I sit like Rodin's
Thinker, thinking

now I pick up
the mala Joy made me
the beads
at my fingertips
counting, counting

midnight
he reaches the mountain
one less worry –
the bears
are in hibernation

I do not think
I ever found my real self
if there is such a thing
I am a series of moments
some good, some not

what would I sing
if people would listen?
'when you walk
through a storm
hold your head up high'

I find
this early waking hour
is not helpful
nor is the early hour
of going to bed and dreaming

how hungry
the mother cat
alone at the bowl
when the young ones come
she holds off and lets them eat

how dark
the world has become
how violent
no words of mine can
come close to saying it

finding
I gained my own space
in the dark world
in it I feel my fall
will be steep, deep

the boy
who gardens
only fifteen
strange to find he is writing
haiku for Blithe Spirit

two worlds –
the positive one
the negative one
I wonder if I can get
out of the horrible second

a mystery to himself,
the hermit writes
when she asks for poems –
lines on ruled paper descending
are they really bringing relief?

the inner world
of an ageing tanka hermit
comes out in fives
perhaps the books he reads help
perhaps his poems bring relief

December fifth
scheduled for execution
my pen-pal for years
no response to my special delivery
is he still alive? is he now dead?

my dreams
are not romantic
sometimes pigs
flying in dreams
would be less frustrating

never
do I look
into sand
stones, sprigs
not in my world

no witches
or ghosts
or old ruins
I have never been
to Norwich

why does
nothing from sea or land
or deserts
flood my old
tired mind?

seldom lately
does any inspiration
come to me
living here and now is
enough for me

I feel
the exhaustion
of dizziness
and still I walk
still I dry dishes

invited
to a wedding
in America
alas, all I can do
is send some cash

reading
my published tanka
I wonder
how can I have been
trivial so often?

my friend
reminds me
of this and that
the forgotten
is entire thick volumes

I have
gone from my native
land
and there is no road
to return

beyond her windows
she looks down on moss
grass, and pink buds
my view from the kitchen entrance
dust rags and an old vacuum

I think
and hope for her
even though
she is happy to eat
wild blueberries

we will be
found or lost
together
let us continue
to strive

old age
has made me forget
and not do things
accurately –
I am an aged twit!

I write strings
only with her
I want to e-mail
her even on
my death bed

quiet walks
and quiet talks
and writing tanka
I am in a whirl
even as I dread being alone

I rely
on her loving rope
to get me
out of the dumps
and ditches

when we die
do we leave energy behind
in the minds of those
who remember us?
maybe ghost tanka?

I am
waiting for the moment
to act
sometimes too close
sometimes too far

at the tanka café
something has changed
after all these years
it's not the café itself
it's a different Sandy

I long to sleep
and sleep more
nowadays
for waking brings
the same routine

unable
to walk lately
without pain
that fall two weeks ago
has lasted days and nights

the long
Trollope novel
I'm reading
one hero I have disliked
about to commit suicide

a long stretch
of loneliness
to endure
I decide to vacuum
my dirty study

how to pass my days
endure my long nights
I bear up
no sign of relief
but my great-grandson is born!

a review
of my book on
Minimalism
the reviewer moves me
to endless tears

what is
the use of this
long life?
the days pass
the nights pass

again
a great-grandfather
am I –
I imagine the lifetime
that boy has to go through

my beard
will never get to
look good
I shave away
my endless regret

tell me
inner withered muse
of my tanka life
where should I go?
when will I leave?

I watch
many young Japanese
returning from school,
the loads they carry
in the pouring rain

loneliness
every way
not stopping
I sit alone and ponder
my nothing world

waiting
for miracles
to happen
of course they avoid
my lonely house

in my tanka café
this cold evening
I have on
my new boots
that keep me from falling

my friend is going
to spend time
at another house
and I will be alone
for three long days

I found
my poems
in a published book …
is it the luck
of the Irish?

no longer
at my former
tanka café
I found a new place
to write my poems

I wandered
but not lonely
as a cloud
I have the company
of my new boots!

will I live
another year
or two? still one year
would be enough
for lonely me

apart
from all my wants
and desires
I go along my silent road
I bear up no matter what

reading
a crime novel
sent by my daughter
I remain lost, unable
to place the characters

again
at my tanka café
again
mediocre poems
spilled without relief

a chill
from the windows
behind me
this coffee shop will serve me
a winter-warm drink

all night
in my narrow bed
I hear sounds,
have the destroyers come?
will I be able to be rescued?

the wife
enters this coffee
shop,
so lovely is she
so wrapped up in life

bewildered in
these days of heat
and loneliness
still the joy of seeing on the screen
my great-grandson walking

tell me,
abandoning muse
of my tanka world
when will you appear
before I disappear?

I have wandered
into barren fields where
no birds fly
I stop to throw stones
at my stream reflection

done
with trivialities
what's next?
nothing more serious
than a gravestone

Sandy & *Joy* strings …

lost

lost in the now
and lost too the memories
of decades,
at the tanka cafe tonight,
perhaps I will spill fifteen

sometimes,
lost in the pain
I forget –
the now of words and songs,
of violins and bells

I prefer losing
my old and battered
wallet,
what I don't want to lose
are the losses that keep coming

my wedding ring
somewhere in the wreckage
on the road –
my sense of safety
and simple faith, lost too

strange again
seeing on a wall the notice
of the lost and found
can it be true that what is lost
can be found in that simple way?

bells

the bell for school
rang and rang again
and I ran,
a buzz instead of a bell
for dismissal saddens me

the high echo
of brass prayer cymbals
in the holy room –
I go outside and face
the wild biting wind

not bells it was,
a knock if I remember so long ago
for the spirit of Christmas past,
these cold days in remote Japan,
John Donne seems to echo in my study

<>

sand and wind

I want now,
now, now–not the past,
not the future, but now –
still, moments of pain from the past
come into the now

missing him
I warm the sake
and light the fire –
hours later I am lost
in another place and time

behind my ears
dust from sand and wind
gathers –
is this the prelude
of my final condition?

I swim deep
in the water; he stands
on the edge
his hand reaching for mine
mine reaching for his

comfort
in these mala beads
and rest too
the counting from bead to bead
makes me see many roads

missing the mark

certain I was
tossing the horseshoe
a ringer confidence
was it the rhythm that foiled me?
was it the logic throwing me off?

thinking I know
the meaning of life
and what I must do –
I get lost in plans and pain
and lose sight of the goal

a hit-and-miss
life is starting again
with the morning chill
not even into the real cold
I fail to settle into wise choices

all night long
unable to sleep
I write tanka –
in the morning, I throw them
one by one on the fire

my friend
misses the lunch call
his coming home late
makes me feel something
has gone wrong in Jerusalem

lines

there are lines
as yet we have not crossed
set boundaries –
day by day in my mind
I'm dismantling the walls

trapped in boundaries
all day and most of the night
and I wait
a small space there is where
a slight opening helps me though

even if
I could pull you through
to another side
still the heavy chains
keep us from flight

the boundary
I find in amazement
is this distance from you
'though the walls be higher each
day
still a slight tug, and I fly

in the old poem
about a Persian beauty
kept behind walls –
her lover sends a small bird
to sing his love to her

limits

so many things
we can no longer do
these hard days –
where do we find
the courage to go on?

when young
the world lay spread
before us
much older now, we find it
closing in and darkening the all

a light goes out
and we stumble, falling
and shaken –
an uncertain tomorrow
lies ahead of us

a weary pace
in this world of limits
of limitations
to want for less may be the
answer
to embrace the limits another
way

my wild dreams
fall by the wayside
turning to dust
and still ... something grows
heading for the light

<>

loneliness

alone
with this lonely self
all day
I bear up and bear up
and still the loneliness goes on

too many
the visitors who come
to my door
I hear the doorbell
ringing in my sleep

no door bells
no friends on my phone
no handshakes
my sleep is my lonely life
shut off from interruptions

over lunch
visitors chatting
I listen
there is a place inside me
where no one comes

enough
of loneliness
for this day
soon soon soon
I will catch up

decay

I am
an old-timer
laid out
to rot
in the sun

without
erosion
and decay
nothing new
can grow

my body
decays
and my mind
so what else
is new?

the soul
emerges
and flies
up, away from
the broken shell

so far, life
defeats
the soul
and I remain
rudderless

<>

window

again
illness enters
our window
again her pain,
again mine

open,
a window
admits air
and light
and the truth

these
dark evenings
one bright window –
the evening e-mail chat
with the Norwich poet

there are
other joys than me
in your life
tell me them
my sad poet-friend

we're upside
down
in this world,
our window is open
wide, free

<>

death's holiday

I was close to death
and suddenly it took
time off
to let me stay
a while longer

hold on
to life old friend
this cold night
the Grim Reaper calls
another man's name

and should mine
be called,
that then?
walking walking
down narrow lanes

keep moving
facing the light
don't look back
the past is gone
the future lies in mist

there's
no looking back
from this old age
the now is always
with me

<>

company

my morning
walk the usual
forty-plus minutes
and as I walk
Joy walks with me

caught
on the sharp horns
of dilemmas
I put some of the weight
in the old man's hands

to help
a friend
is not a weight
I wait only for
your escape from pain

it may be
a long hard journey
my friend
there are no road signs –
how far can you walk?

the journey
may be hard
may be long
you can do it
and so can I

<>

you

you
will be
with me
to the end
of my life

the tomb
may be cold
and dark
but see, ahead
a small light

I see
no after-world
still
even a spark
lights the dark

breathe
on the ashes –
see?
orange
inside the grey

orange
grey
blue –
no matter
you remain with me

<>

Threads

unable
to find the energy
for tanka
I still want to do strings
with my favorite person

those threads
between us
will hold
strong silk
blowing in the wind

at times
my own silk blown
in a Japanese wind
may a few days this month
be even more windy

wild storms
batter my land
still, the strings
that hold us fast
do not break

our world
a together string
we lean in wind or rain
and still our string
endures

the unknown

never
do we know
what lies
around the corner
we take small steps

every corner
nowadays contains
the unknown,
more and more uncertainty
in our violent world

here and there
now and then, a gentle light
on the pathway
and for a moment
the darkness retreats

the temporary
darkness may retreat
returning in a flash
I sit back and watch the world
turning, turning, to darkness

oh my friend
remember the coin
do not despair
behind every shadow
there is sunshine

patches

fabric scraps
of soft handerchiefs
your long ago gift –
patches on my skirts
my pillows, my life

to think of
the handkerchiefs
long ago given to you,
it is an important patch
in my life

it's the thread
that holds everything
sewn together
until time and death
make the stiches unravel

<>

shadow

leaves
on the Japanese mountain
age and turn yellow
why am I not a yellow
walking shadow on this hill?

in the mirror
looking back at me
not smiling –
a woman with white hair
and sad grey eyes

render me stoic
you forces
in a world of contra-
I do not walk with fists
I wimp my old age through

can I be
indifferent to pain
and ageing?
no stoic, I want it all
the sharp grief, the shining joy

at times
I see the uselessness
of age,
what remains for the pathos
is this limping along

<>

leaving

and still
I know what and where
happiness can be
let the slips and stains
be where they lie as I limp
on

it is time
to leave behind me
old futile dreams –
the tree does not despair
when the leaves have
fallen

so absent-minded
nowadays in my dizzy
spasms
memory seems to be buried
in the ugly slush on
sidewalks

a long splash
of dark blood in the snow
and fox footprints –
these small wild deaths sting
more than my own wounds

what's this new feeling
at the tanka café
where I wrote poems –
as if, as if, I am abandoned
a life gone if I leave Japan

pieces

that precious dish
pushed with an elbow
fell to the floor
the boy of fifteen came for hours
and puzzling, made it whole

so quiet
his ways and his voice
beside me –
he mends the shattered dish
he cannot mend his broken dreams

pieces
of logic float into
my mind;
now quite as lost as Job
I have to see what I can do right

the mongrel dogs
outside the gate with Job
licked his sores –
sometimes my help too
comes from unlikely places

like trying
to put a jigsaw puzzle
together
this gathering of thoughts from here
and from there and the unknown

grim spirits

may the Norwich ghosts
return to your house
and remain
let them ease your pain
let them ease you into joy

there are spirits
some grim, some merry
in these cobbled streets –
still, I find more comfort
in your living friendship

when I was
in elementary school in Ohio,
a sign warned me:
do not pick any flowers!
I feared a witch would fly out

'step on a crack,
break your mother's back'
said the old rhyme –
in Shibata-shi or Norwich
still those childhood terrors

out on Halloween
for trick or treat in big bags
with my kids,
how the treats piled up, and still...
the bad witch put pins in the apples

distant distances

he writes
'thoughts from abroad'
and at once
the only distance
between us is in miles

that woolen sock
you put on
only last night
the warmth grabbed me
and made me glad for you

the old hermit
dyed in the wool
of solitude –
from a thousand miles away
speaks in my quiet room

from China
the pollution drifts in
and stains our air
I see peasants in the crowded streets
vision a blur, mouths unable to open

are we dumb
in the face of ignorance?
are we deaf
to the voice of reason?
are we blind to love?

<>

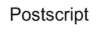

Postscript

I will
endure to the end
of my time,
and still the end remains
ambiguous

I tried
to walk this morning
but failed.
I rest on my couch
like an exhausted old man

my supper's
being made at
the tanka cafe,
and these tanka too
spill on the page

I see
how the world
is breaking,
global warming
is a sad sad joke

how violent
the morning rain,
down and down and down,
the pancakes beside me
and I wait to pick up my spoon

where
has the young man
disappeared?
he used to come to
the café but no longer

what to do?
how to go on
in this dreary world?
I decide to stay put,
and try to live my life out

Sanford Goldstein

for Kazuaki

sometimes
the winds were cold, severe,
sometimes the rooms dark,
and still my soulmate came late
and still he remained at my side

Sandy

from: Journeys Near and Far
© by Sanford Goldstein 2013

Tribute tanka from Kazuaki Wakui, artist
and Sandy's housemate at Atellib House,
Shibata-shi. May 2023

the very first night
after he left
so cold, so dark with nobody
will he back late?
will he still be on my side?

yes, friend
from the distance
you sat so close to him
his being in the process of loss
in the deepest sadness

with a touch
crystal pyramid for the farewell
burst into pieces
and spread over the floor
like stars out of the blue

as it happens
as it follows
everything in life
eventually turns in to a gem
by the poet's magic

finally
I've found my place
as a grave keeper
who connects the living with the dead
who connects the wounded with healers

what is tanka
you'd have written all about this?
deeply held the answer
in the cerulean blue of the sky of May
he has gone without a word forever

<>